E

Questions and Answers

MATHEMATICS

KEY STAGE 4

Mark Patmore Senior Examiner
Brian Seager Chief Examiner

SERIES EDITOR: BOB McDUELL

Contents

HOW TO USE THIS BOOK

The aim of the *Questions and Answers* series is to provide the student with the help required to attain the highest level of achievement in one of their most important examinations – the General Certificate of Secondary Education (GCSE). The books are designed to help all students including up to A* grade: questions, or part questions, at this level will be indicated with a *, and in the Revision Summaries, statements or comments for A* will be shown as *[.............]*. The material in this book also provides a good basis for revision for the Standard Grade of the Scottish Certificate of Education, General and Credit Levels.

The series relies on the premise that an experienced Examiner can provide, through examination questions, sample answers and advice, the help a student needs to secure success. Many revision aids concentrate on providing factual information which might have to be recalled in an examination. This series, while giving factual information in an easy to remember form, concentrates on the other skills which need to be developed for GCSE examinations.

Students often find it useful to plan their revision according to some predetermined pattern, during which weaknesses can be identified and eliminated so that confidence can grow, and so the primary consideration has been to present the main principles on which study can be based.

The *Questions and Answers* series is designed to provide:

- Easy to use **Revision Summaries** which identify important factual information. These are to remind you, in summary form, of the topics you will need to have revised in order to answer exam questions. (Answers to the illustrative examples are also provided.)

- Advice on the different types of question in each subject and how to answer them well to obtain the highest marks.

- Many examples of **examination questions**, with spaces for you to fill in your answers, just as in an examination. A student can improve by studying a sufficiently wide range of questions providing they are shown the way to improve their answers to those questions. It is advisable that students try the questions first before going to the answers and the advice which accompanies the answers. The questions have been written by experienced Examiners who write questions for Examination Boards. The questions meet the requirements of all British Examination Boards.

- **Sample answers** to all of the questions.

- **Advice from Examiners**. By using the experience of Examiners we are able to give advice which can enable the student to see how their answers can be improved and success be ensured.

Success in GCSE examinations comes from proper preparation and a positive attitude to the examination developed through a sound knowledge of facts and an understanding of principles. These books are intended to overcome 'examination nerves' which often come from a fear of not being properly prepared.

DEVISING A REVISION PLAN

The importance of beginning your revision well in advance of your examination cannot be overemphasized. You will obtain a fair idea of your memory capacity by reading a part of a text which is new to you and, after 40 minutes, writing out how many facts you can remember. The average person will recall about 50%, then after an interval of 10 minutes, 25% of the original material will be remembered. After two days you will probably recall no more than 15%. These are average figures of course, so do not be depressed if your scores are lower or complacent if they are higher. Your capacity for retention will be influenced by the amount of sleep that you have had, what other matters are on your mind and your interest in the topic.

The fact that only 15% of the material you learn may be remembered could be depressing and make you wonder whether revision is worthwhile. What is important, however, is that the amount remembered is dramatically increased by revising the original material after one week and then again after two weeks. By this time the facts will be stored in your so-called long-term memory store and up to 80% of the original material should be retained.

You can only maintain concentration for a short period of time and the actual amount of time will vary from person to person. Break up your revision into short periods of time, perhaps 30 minutes or so each and build in short breaks between revision periods. Set yourself a reasonable target for each week – something that you can achieve but will stretch you. Monitor your progress and amend your weekly targets accordingly. Divide the topics to be studied into two lists – ones you need to work on and ones you are happy with. Try to transfer as many as possible from the first list into the second.

DIFFERENT TYPES OF EXAMINATION QUESTION

There are different types of examination questions which appear on examination papers. Questions on mathematics papers are of two types:

'Pure' Mathematics Questions

These are usually short and are focused on one particular skill or part of the syllabus.
Questions of this type could be:

Example 1: solve the equation $x^2 - 3x - 40 = 0$.

Example 2: find the angles marked with the letters a and b. O is the centre of the circle, AT is a tangent and AB a diameter.

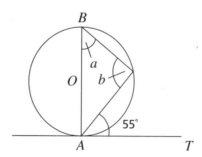

Structured Questions

These are perhaps the most common type of question at the higher levels of GCSE on Mathematics papers and thus most of the questions in this book are structured questions. These questions usually have a context – that is they are about the application of mathematics to a real (or nearly real!) situation.

In a structured question, the question is divided into parts (a), (b), (c) etc. These parts may be further subdivided into (i), (ii) and so on. A structure is built into the question and, hence, into your answer. Frequently, answers from one part of a question are used in subsequent parts, but an error in, say, part (a), which may result in few, or even no, marks being obtained for that part should not result in no marks being obtained in subsequent parts, provided the incorrect answer is used 'correctly'. There are numbers in brackets, e.g. (3), to show how many marks are allocated to the various parts of a question.

Questions of this type could be:

Example 3: (a) astronomers estimate that there are about one thousand million galaxies in the universe. Write this figure in standard form.

Answer (a) ___ 1×10^{9} ___ (2)

(b) each galaxy contains about one hundred thousand million stars. Write this figure in standard form.

Answer (b) _____ (2)

(c) use your answers to parts (a) and (b) to estimate the number of stars in the universe. Write your answer in standard form.

Answer (c) _____ (3)

Example 4: the diagram shows the design for a company's logo which is to be painted on the side of a building.

The design is a rectangle, *ABCD*, 10 m long and 6 m wide. *E*, the midpoint of *AD*, and *F*, the midpoint of *DC*, are joined to *B*. *XY* is the line joining the midpoints of *BF* and *BC*. Triangles *ABE* and *BXY* are painted yellow. Quadrilaterals *BEDF* and *XYFC* are painted red and blue, respectively.

(a) calculate the area of triangle *ABE*

Answer (a) _____ m² (3)

(b) calculate the area of triangle *BFC*

Answer (b) _____ m² (3)

(c) hence calculate the area of quadrilateral *BEDF*

Answer (c) _____ m² (3)

(d) calculate the areas of triangle *BXY* and trapezium *XYCF*

Answer (d) _____ m², _____ m² (4)

One litre of paint will cover 12 m².

(e) Calculate the volume of red, blue and yellow paint needed.

Answer (e) red _____ litres (3)

blue _____ litres

yellow _____ litres

Answers to examples:
1: $x = 8$ or $x = -5$
2: angle $a = 55°$, angle $b = 90°$
3: (a) 10^9 (b) 10^{11} (c) 10^{20}
4: (a) 15 m²   (b) 15 m²   (c) 30 m²
   (d) triangle *BXY* 3.75 m², trapezium *XYCF* 11.25 m²
   (e) red = 2.5 litres, blue = 0.94 litres, yellow = 1.56 litres.

Note: The mark allocations are only given as a rough guide. They will vary according to the level of the paper on which the questions are set.

1 Number

Questions asked in Number, and the knowledge and skills required to answer them fall into three broad categories.

The first is **calculation** and is relatively straightforward. Questions here will involve the manipulation of numbers – the 4 rules ($+$, $-$, $\times$, $\div$) – and the use of calculators. At the lower levels questions such as:

> Example 1: Find the cost of 75 calculators at £8.49 each.

> Example 2: A washing machine has its price reduced from £325 to £280 in a sale. Calculate the percentage reduction.

may be set. At the higher levels the questions may include topics such as standard form:

> Example 3: If $x = 1.4 \times 10^{-3}$ and $y = 4.6 \times 10^4$ find, in standard form, (a) $x \times y$, and (b) $x \div y$.

Substitution into a formula may be required:

> Example 4: If $\dfrac{1}{f} = \dfrac{1}{u} + \dfrac{1}{v}$ find f when $u = 2$ and $v = 3$.

The next group of questions are concerned with **estimation**, **approximation** and **errors**. Questions involving **estimation** may ask for answers to be checked and/or justified.

> Example 5: Show that the value of $\dfrac{17.8 \times 0.53}{0.238}$ is roughly 40.

This is a useful way to check all work on the calculator.

Questions involving **approximation** could include some which asked for answers to be rounded to appropriate degrees of accuracy as well as those involving calculations using approximate numbers. **Errors** arise in questions where, for example, measurements to a given degree of accuracy are involved.

> Example 6: 27.3 is correct to 3 significant figures. Write the upper and lower bounds.

[Determining the possible effects of error on calculations] This could be demonstrated by:

> * Example 7: If $s = ut + \frac{1}{2}at^2$ find the largest and smallest value that s could have when $u = 5.6$, $t = 4.3$ and $a = 9.8$, if these values are correct to 1 decimal place.

The last group of questions involve the identification and manipulation of **irrational numbers** and comparisons between rational and irrational numbers, for example: $\dfrac{1}{\sqrt{2}}$ is an irrational number but $\left(\dfrac{1}{\sqrt{2}}\right)^2 = \dfrac{1}{2}$ is rational.

If you need to revise this subject more thoroughly, see the relevant topics in the *Letts* GCSE Mathematics Study Guide.

Answers to examples:

1: £636.75	2: 13.8%	3: (a) 6.44×10 (b) 3.04×10^{-8}
4: 1.2	6: 27.25 and 27.35	* 7: largest is 117.7, smallest is 111.7

(N.B. Answer for largest must be less than the upper bound; answer for smallest must be greater than the lower bound. More than 4 significant figures is unreasonable.)

1   Mrs Jones bought 40 scientific calculators costing £7.30 each and some graphical calculators costing £36.80 each. Altogether she spent £733.60. How many graphical calculators did she buy?

....

Answer _____ (2)

2   During the first 3 weeks of life a baby increases its weight from 3.6 kg to 4.7 kg. What is the percentage increase?

....

Answer _____% (2)

3   There are about 7000 cinemas in the UK. Every day about 400 people visit each one. The population of the UK is about 60 million. About what percentage of the population visit a cinema each day?

....

Answer _____% (2)

4

A car manufacturer reduces the prices of its hatchback from £12 800 to £12 400. What is the percentage reduction?

....

....

Answer _____ % (2)

5   If $V = IR$, what is the percentage increase in V when I increases by 10% and R increases by 20%?

....

....

Answer _____ % (4)

6 The land area of the Earth's surface is about 4×10^{11} km². The population of the Earth is approximately 5000 million.

(a) Write the population of the Earth in standard form.

Answer _____ (1)

(b) Calculate the approximate average area, in km² per head of population. Give your answer in standard form.

....

Answer _____ km² (2)

7 If $P = \sqrt{\dfrac{V}{Q}}$, find P when $V = 4.6 \times 10^6$ and $Q = 2.8 \times 10^2$. Give your answer in standard form.

....

Answer $P =$ _____ (2)

8 Calculate:

(a) $\dfrac{26.78 \times 0.0831}{15.3 \times 6.81}$

(i) Show all the digits on your calculator display.

Answer _____ (2)

(ii) Round your answer to a sensible degree of accuracy.

Answer _____ (1)

(b) $\dfrac{15.32 + 9.07}{15.32 - 9.07}$

Show all the digits.

....

Answer _____ (2)

9 Henry bought some furniture. It cost £1750.

(a) The shop offered him credit as follows:

Repayment over 12 months

Cash	10% deposit	Monthly payments	Total credit price
1750.00	175.00	147.00 *1764*	1939.00

He paid the 10% deposit. What is the rate of interest on the amount to be repaid?

....

Answer _____% (2)

(b) He could have paid back the money over 2 years:

Repayment over 24 months

Cash	10% deposit	Monthly payments	Total credit price
1750.00	175.00	81.37	2127.88

Show how you can **estimate** whether this is the same rate of interest per year.

.... (2)

10 I have a small packet to post. To find out how much it will cost, I weigh it.

(a) First I weigh it on scales that weigh to the nearest 10 g.
The packet weighs 70 g.

Write down the smallest that the weight of the packet could be.

Answer _____ *65* _____ g (1)

7

(b) Now I weigh it on electronic scales where the display goes up in 5 g intervals. The packet weighs 65 g.

Write down the upper and lower bounds of the weight of the package according to the electronic scales.

Upper bound .... g   Lower bound .... g   (2)

(c) Finally, I weigh it on a balance to the nearest gram. It weighs 62 g.

Can all the scales be right? Explain.

.... (2)

11 The formula

$$s = \frac{v^2 - u^2}{2a}$$

gives the distance travelled in metres when the velocity changes from u m/s to v m/s due to a constant acceleration of a m/s^2.

Find s when

$v = 25.0$
$u = 50.0$
$a = -9.8$

....

Answer $s =$ _____ m (3)

12 Angela is going to sow grass seed on a small field. She has estimated the lengths of the sides (in metres) and the angles shown in the diagram:

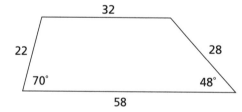

(a) Show that the field is approximately a trapezium.

....

.... (5)

*(b) All the measurements are correct to the nearest whole number. Angela has seed for 1000 m^2. Can she be sure that this is enough? Show your calculation.

....

.... (4)

13 Mr Clark borrowed £650 on 1 January 1990. He repaid £243 on 31 December 1990 and the same amount each succeeding 31 December. Compound interest was charged at 6% per annum on the balance during the year. How much was left to pay after 31 December 1992?

....

Answer £ _____ (3)

*14 Kris ran a 400 m race in 49.4 seconds. If the time was measured to the nearest 0.1 seconds and the distance is measured to the nearest metre, what is the maximum value of his average speed, in metres per second?

....

....

Answer _____ m/s (3)

15 Some of these numbers are irrational. In each case, show how you decided whether it was rational or irrational.

(a) 3.142

.... (1)

(b) $1.\dot{6}$

.... (1)

(c) $(\sqrt{3})^3$

.... (2)

(d) $(1 + \sqrt{3})(1 - \sqrt{3})$

.... (2)

(e) $\dfrac{1 + \sqrt{3}}{1 - \sqrt{3}}$

.... (3)

2 Algebra

* indicates grade A* level material

Questions asked in algebra and the knowledge and skills required to answer them fall into three broad categories.

The first is **number patterns and sequences**. It will be necessary to find rules which enable you to continue a number pattern such as 1, 3, 6, 10, 15, ... in words or symbols. *[Investigations to determine whether a sequence converges or diverges will also be needed. This could involve other algebraic skills.]*

The next group of questions is the largest and involves **solving equations and algebraic manipulation**. At the simplest level it will be necessary to solve equations such as:

Example 1: (a) $5x - 3 = 3 - x$ or (b) $x^2 = 27$

the latter by the method of 'trial and improvement'. More complex equations will also be set. An equation such as

Example 2: $x^2 + 2x = 7$

can also be solved by trial and improvement *[also by the use of the quadratic formula, completing the square or by iteration]*. Graphical methods may also be used, possibly associated with other mathematics. Equations like

Example 3: $2x - y = 9$
$x + 3y = 8$

may be solved by graphical or algebraic methods. In addition to equations, inequalities must also be solved. These can range from listing whole numbers which satisfy, for example:

Example 4: $-2 < n \leqslant 6$

to finding values of x and y which satisfy

Example 5: $x > 7, y \geqslant 4, x + y \leqslant 20$

Again, solution by graphical or algebraic methods may be required. Such solutions will involve algebraic manipulation but the factorizing of expressions such as

Example 6: (a) $ax^2 + 2bx$ or (b) $x^2 - 3x - 10$

will occur either as part of a longer question or on their own. Expanding (multiplying out brackets), is another skill that could be required and 'changing the subject' of a formula is a regular requirement.

Example 7: make a the subject of $v = u + at$

[More complicated algebraic manipulation will be expected which could include algebraic fractions but these will usually be in context and not asked merely to test the skill]

The last group is concerned with **graphical representation**. The use of coordinates is expected at all levels and this may involve graphical solutions as already mentioned. The interpretation of graphs of simple functions and also those which represent physical situations, such as speed/time, will be asked. *[Comparing the graphs of related functions could be required and also sketching the graphs of derived functions, given the graph of the original function.]* Finding and using gradients of graphs found by drawing tangents is a further skill. *[And also finding the approximate area between a curve, the axis and two limits, interpreting the result, as when the area under an acceleration/time curve can give velocity.]*

If you need to revise this subject more thoroughly, see the relevant topics in the *Letts* GCSE *Mathematics Study Guide.*

Answers to examples:

1: (a) $x = 1$ (b) $x = 5.2$ or -5.2 2: $x = 1.8$ or -3.8 3: $x = 5, y = 1$

4: $-1, 0, 1, 2, 3, 4, 5, 6$ 5: many answers possible, for example if $x = 8$ then y would lie between 4 and 12.

6: (a) $x(ax + 2b)$ (b) $(x - 5)(x + 2)$ 7: $a = \dfrac{v - u}{t}$

Letts
Q&A

1 The first 3 terms of a sequence are:

$(3 \times 4) + 1$, $(4 \times 5) + 2$, $(5 \times 6) + 3$.

(a) Write down the next term.

.... (1)

(b) Write down the 6th term.

.... (1)

(c) Write down the nth term, and simplify your answer.

.... (3)

2 Look at this sequence

$$3,\ 6,\ 11,\ 18,\ 27,\ ...$$

(a) (i) Write down the next two terms in the sequence.

....

Answer _____ (1)

(ii) Explain how you would find the next term.

.... (1)

(b) Find an expression for the nth term of

(i) $1,\ 4,\ 9,\ 16,\ 25,\ ...$

....

Answer _____ (1)

(ii) $3,\ 6,\ 11,\ 18,\ 27,\ ...$

....

Answer _____ (2)

3 $1,\ 2,\ 1\frac{1}{2},\ 1\frac{3}{4},\ 1\frac{5}{8},\ \uparrow\frac{7}{32}$

(a) Explain how to get the next term.

.... (1)

*(b) Investigate whether or not this sequence converges and, if it does, find the limit.

....

Answer _____ (4)

4 (a) Multiply out the brackets and simplify the expression $(2x + 7)(3x - 6)$.

....

Answer _____ (2)

(b) (i) Factorize $x^2 + x - 6$.

....

(ii) Solve the equation $x^2 + x - 6 = 0$.

....

Answer $x =$ _____ (4)

5 Solve the equations:

(a) $11 - 3x = 4x - 10$,

....

Answer $x =$ _____ (3)

(b) $x^3 = 7$.
   Use trial and improvement and show all your trials. Give your answer correct to 2 decimal places.

....

Answer $x =$ _____ (4)

6 Freda wants to make a run for her rabbits. She has a roll of netting 22 m long and is going to use it to make three sides of a rectangle. The other side will be part of the garden fence. The length of the side at right angles to the fence is x m. The area inside will be 60 m².

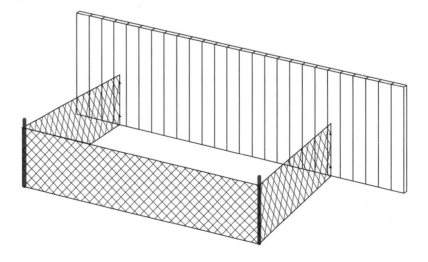

(a) Show that $x^2 - 11x + 30 = 0$.

.... (3)

*(b) Solve the equation.

....

....

Answer $x = $ _____ (3)

(c) Describe the size of the run.

.... (2)

7 John and Sayed are playing a number game:

I think of
a number, multiply
it by 3 and subtract 4

Is the
answer less
than 17?

yes

Let n be the number John thought of.

(a) Write down the inequality using n.

....

Answer _____ (1)

(b) Solve the inequality.

....

Answer _____ (2)

8 Find, by trial and improvement, the positive solution of $x^2 - x = 11$ giving your answer to 2 decimal places.

....

....

Answer _____ (4)

Letts

Q&A

9 Solve the simultaneous equations: $2x + 3y = 17$
$3x - 2y = 6.$

....

....

Answer $x =$ _____ $y =$ _____ (4)

10 The sum of the squares of the integers from 1 to n is given by

$$s = \frac{1}{6} n (n + 1)(2n + 1).$$

Find s when $n = 10$.

....

Answer $s =$ _____ (2)

11

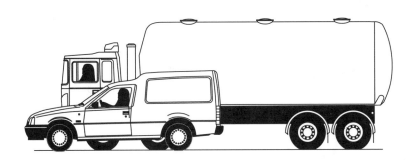

The traffic capacity of a road can be found by using the following formula:

$$Q = \frac{3600VN}{C}$$

Q = number of vehicles per hour
V = average speed in m/s
N = number of lanes
C = optimum distance between vehicles

(a) Find the capacity of a 2 lane road where the average speed is 12 m/s and the optimum distance is 55 m.

....

Answer $Q =$ _____ (2)

(b) How many lanes will be needed through a tunnel which will have to take 1000 vehicles an hour, travelling at 15m/s with a spacing of 120 m?

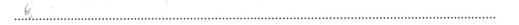

Answer $N =$ _____ (3)

12 To change from Fahrenheit to Celsius we use the formula:

$$C = \tfrac{5}{9}(F - 32)$$

John claims that, on a hot day, the Fahrenheit reading can be exactly double the Celsius reading. At what temperature, Celsius, would this be true?

....

....

Answer _____ °C (4)

13 The mean and the median of the following numbers are equal. Find x.

30, 40, x, 50, 80.

....

....

Answer $x =$ _____ (5)

14 The *Better Diary Service* supply two kinds of desk diary, the *Page per Day* (PPD) and the *Page per Week* (PPW).
These are two of the orders:

3 PPD	7 PPW	Total cost	£53.40
1 PPD	10 PPW	Total cost	£50.00

Let d be the price of one PPD in £
w be the price of one PPW in £.

(a) Write down two equations in d and w.

.... (2)

(b) Solve the equations to find the cost of each diary.

....

....

Answer PPD .... PPW .... (4)

15 Write down all the whole numbers (n) which satisfy

$$-1 < n \leq 3.$$

.... (2)

16 Mr Brick the builder owns a plot of land, *ABCD*. The dimensions are in metres.

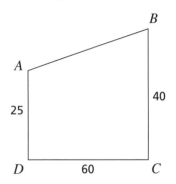

Not to scale

He decides that it is big enough for two houses. He wants to divide it so that the areas of the two parts are equal. The dividing line *EF* must be parallel to *AD* and *BC*. *DF* = *x*.

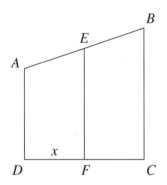

(a) Explain why $EF = 25 + \frac{1}{4}x$.

.... (2)

(b) Show that *x* satisfies the equation

$$x^2 + 200x - 7800 = 0.$$

....

.... (3)

(c) Solve the equation to find the length of *DF*. Give your answer to the nearest 0.1 m.

....

....

Answer *x* = _____ (3)

(d) Explain how you know your answer is about right.

.... (1)

17

An old formula gives the distance D miles that can be seen to the horizon when the observer is at height h feet above the sea. The radius of the Earth is r miles and is equal to 3950.

$$D = \sqrt{\frac{2rh}{5280}}$$

Find h when $D = 20$.

....

....

Answer $h = $ _____ feet   (3)

18 Boyle's Law can be stated by the formula

$$P = \frac{k}{V}$$

where P is the pressure and V the volume of a gas.
Transform the formula to make V the subject.

....   (2)

19 Solve the inequalities

(a) $2x - 7 \leqslant 8$.

....

Answer _____   (1)

(b) $3 - x > 2$.

....

Answer _____   (1)

(c) $x^2 - 4 < 0$.

....

Answer _____   (2)

20 The area of a rectangle is $6 \, \text{m}^2$. If the diagonal is $\sqrt{13} \, \text{m}$ long what are the dimensions of the rectangle?

....

....

Answer _____ m by _____ m (6)

21 I want to make a regular octagon. Each side will be 14 cm. I shall make it from a square piece of card, by cutting off the four corners.

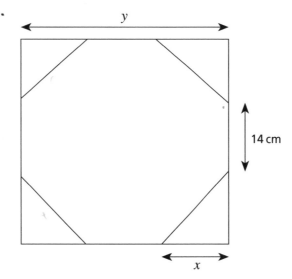

(a) Write down an expression for the area of the octagon in terms of x and y.

....

Answer Area = _____ (2)

(b) Use Pythagoras to find the value of x.

....

....

Answer $x =$ _____ (3)

(c) Find the area of the octagon.

....

....

Answer Area = _____ cm^2 (2)

22 These are the stopping distances for cars at various speeds on a dry road:

Speed (s miles/hour)	30	50	70
Stopping distance (d feet)	75	175	315

There is a formula connecting d and s.

(a) Show that it is not linear.

....

.... (1)

(b) Show that d is not proportional to s^2.

....

.... (1)

(c) The formula is $d = ts + ks^2$. Find the values of t and k.

....

....

Answer $t = $ _____ $k = $ _____ (5)

23 Write these expressions as simply as possible, using index notation:

(a) $x \sqrt{x}$ (b) $\dfrac{1}{x^2}$ (c) $(x^3 y^2)^2$

....

....

Answer (a) _____ (b) _____ (c) _____ (3)

24 On the axes below draw the graphs of

(a) $y = 4 - x$

(b) $y = x^2$

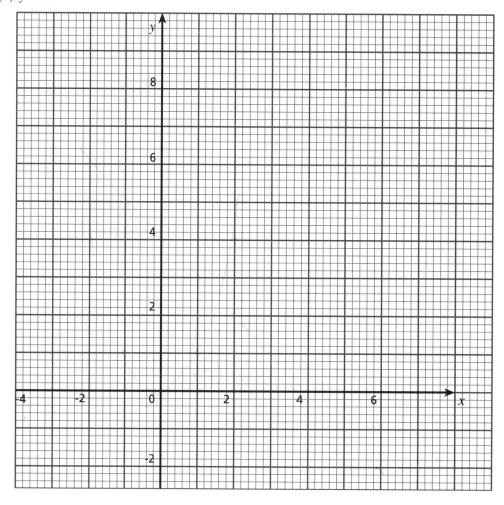

(3)

(c) (i) Write down the values of x where the graphs meet.

Answer $x = $ _____ (2)

(ii) Use trial and improvement to find these solutions correct to 2 decimal places.

....

....

....

Answer $x = $ _____ (4)

25

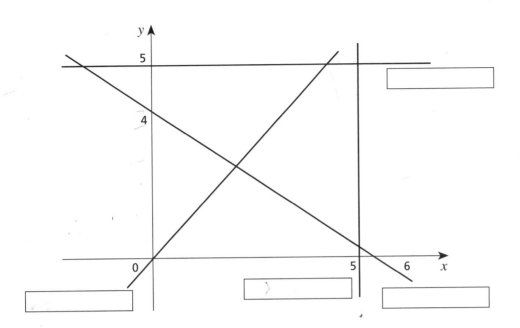

Four lines are drawn on the graph:

$$x = 5, \quad y = 5, \quad 2x + 3y = 12, \quad 2y = 3x.$$

(a) Label the lines by writing the correct equation in each box. (2)

(b) Show, by shading, the region which satisfies

$$x < 5, \quad y < 5, \quad 2x + 3y > 12, \quad 2y < 3x.$$ (2)

26 Match each description to a possible sketch graph. In each case label the axes.

A: $y = x^2$ B: $y = x^3$ C: $y = \dfrac{1}{x}$ D: $y + x = 3$

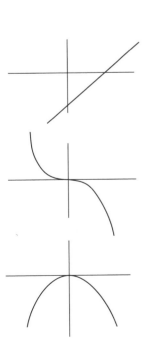
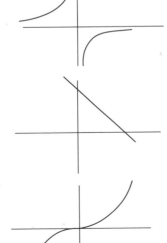
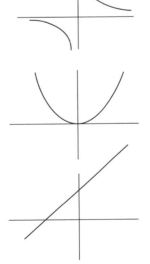

(4)

27 This graph shows the speed of a cyclist as she rides along a hilly road.

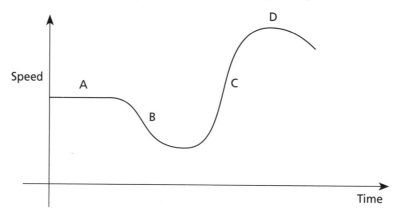

Describe what is happening at A, B, C, D.

A: ....

B: ....

C: ....

D: .... (4)

28

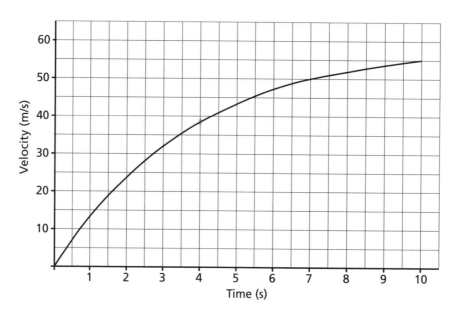

This graph shows the velocity of a sports car starting from rest.

(a) Find the acceleration at time $t = 4$. State the units in your answer.

....

Answer _____ (3)

*(b) Estimate how far the car has travelled during the first 10 seconds.
Make your method clear.

....

Answer _____ m   (4)

*29 The sketch shows the graph of the function

$$y = f(x).$$

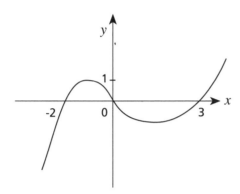

On the diagrams below, sketch the graphs of:

$y = f(x) + 2$ $y = f(x + 2)$

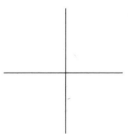   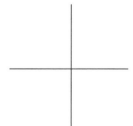

$y = f(x) - 3$ $y = f(x - 3)$

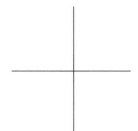   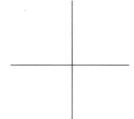

(4)

3 Shape and space

There are three main groups of questions in this attainment target plus some other types of question at the higher levels.

The first group is those concerned with **Pythagoras' Theorem and trigonometry in 2-D and 3-D shapes**.

Here questions such as:

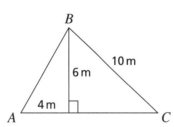

Example 1: Find the length of the sides *AC* and *AB* and the size of the angle *BCA* in the following triangle.

* indicates grade A* level material

could appear but are often set in a context. *[There is a need to recognize the graphs of the sine, cosine and tangent functions for all angles, and to be able to solve problems in non-right-angled triangles using sine and cosine rules, including simple cases in 3-D.]*

The next group involves the calculation of **areas and volumes of 2-D and 3-D shapes**.

You are expected to know the formulae for the area and circumference of a circle ($A = \pi r^2$, $C = 2\pi r$ or πd) and will be given the formulae for the areas and volumes of shapes such as the trapezium, cone and sphere.

Example 2: A child's clown toy is made from a cone attached to a hemisphere of radius 5 cm. If the total height of the toy is 20 cm find its volume.

The third group of questions are those concerned with **position**. These will include bearings – to define direction – and the use of coordinates in two and three dimensions to locate position.

Example 3: A cuboid has its edges parallel to the axes. Its dimensions are 3, 2, 1 units. One vertex is at (2, 3, 0). Find a possible position for the opposite vertex.

The final – mixed – group will include questions concerned with **geometry** for example:

● the conditions for congruent triangles;

● using the laws of addition and subtraction of vectors;

● enlarging shapes and calculating surface area and volume of similar shapes
[the angle and tangent properties of circles; using matrices to define transformations in 2-D; understanding how transformations are related by combinations and inverses.]

If you need to revise this subject more thoroughly, see the relevant topics in the *Letts* GCSE *Mathematics* Study Guide.

*Example 4: A square has coordinates (1,1), (1,2), (2,1), (2,2). It is transformed under matrix $\begin{pmatrix} 1 & -1 \\ 1 & 1 \end{pmatrix}$.

Write down the coordinates of its new position.

Answers to examples:

1: *AB* = 7.2 cm; AC = 12 cm; angle BCA = 36.9°   2: Volume = 654 cm³
3: e.g.: (0, 0, 1), but many others.   *4: (0, 2),(−1, 3),(1, 3),(0, 4)

1 The flag of the Black and White Shipping Company consists of a black rhombus on a white rectangle, as shown in the diagram. The length of the rectangle is 1.6 m, the width is 0.8 m and the rhombus is made by joining the midpoints of the sides.

Calculate the area of material needed to make the black rhombus.

0.8 m

1.6 m

....

....

Answer _____ m² (3)

2 The logo for a company consists of 2 small circles inside a larger circle, as shown. The two inside circles have radii of 2 cm and 3 cm.

(a) Find the radius of the large circle.

....

Answer _____ cm (2)

(b) Find the shaded area.

....

....

Answer _____ cm² (3)

3 Two circular discs are cut out of a rectangular sheet of metal. What is the area of metal left?

6 cm

....

Answer _____ cm² (5)

4   The bottom of this swimming pool slopes evenly from a depth of 2 m at the shallow end to 4 m at the deep end.

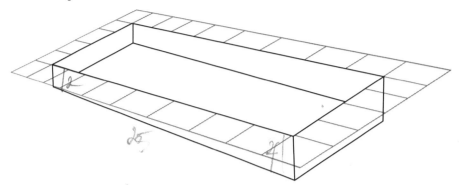

The pool is 25 m long and 15 m wide. Find its volume.

....

....

....

Answer _____ m³ (4)

5   How many spherical balls of radius 1 cm can be made from a large spherical ball of 3 cm radius?

....

....

Answer _____ (2)

6   A semi-circle is cut away from a rectangular piece of metal. The rectangle has length $3r$ cm and width $2r$ cm. Find the area of metal remaining.

2r cm

3r cm

....

....

Answer _____ cm² (4)

7 A lampshade is made by removing the top *VCA* from a hollow cone *VDB* of height 36 cm as shown. The diameter *DB* at the base of the cone is 30 cm and the diameter, *AC*, of the base of the cone removed is 10 cm.

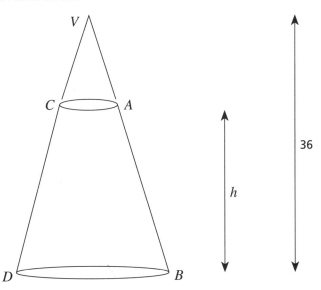

(a) Find the height *h* of the lampshade.

....

....

....

Answer _____ cm (3)

(b) Find the area of the material needed to cover the lampshade.

....

....

....

Answer _____ cm² (6)

Area of curved surface of a cone = πrl

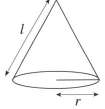

8 The diagram shows a running track with the 'straights' 90 m long and with semicircular end sections. If the inside distance is 400 m and the track is 8 m wide, how much further is it to run round the outside of the track?

....

....

....

Answer _____ m   (5)

9

A new tube of toothpaste is roughly a cylinder, diameter 3.0 cm, length 14.5 cm.

(a) Calculate the volume of toothpaste in the tube.

....

....

Answer _____ cm³   (2)

The toothpaste is squeezed through a circular hole, diameter 7 mm. Each time I clean my teeth, I use a 'cylinder' of length 15 mm.

(b) How many times can I clean my teeth from this tube?

....

....

....

Answer _____   (4)

10 Brian has a photograph measuring 135 mm by 90 mm. It is enlarged until the shorter side is 110 mm.

(a) How long is the other side?

....

....

Answer _____ mm (2)

The cost of printing a photograph is proportional to its area. The smaller one costs 7p.

(b) How much will the larger one cost?

....

....

....

Answer _____ p (3)

11 Find the unknown lengths in these right-angled triangles.

(a)

?   14

8

....

....

....

....

Answer _____ (3)

(b)

7

?

6

....

....

....

....

Answer _____ (3)

DO NOT USE THIS
LADDER AT ANGLES
MORE THAN 70° TO
THE HORIZONTAL

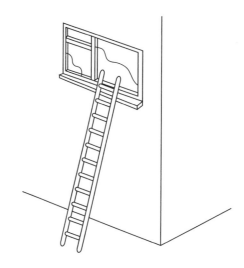

Gurpal's ladder is 5.50 m long.

(a) If it stands on horizontal ground, how far up the wall can it reach?

....

....

Answer _____ m (3)

(b) How far will the foot of the ladder then be from the wall?

....

....

Answer _____ m (3)

Mark also has a ladder. Its length can be extended. He puts his ladder with the foot 1.80 m from the wall. It makes an angle of 67° with the ground.

(c) How far up the wall will it reach?

....

....

Answer _____ m (3)

13 Find the heights of these isosceles triangles.

(a)

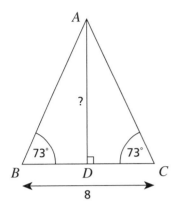

....

....

....

....

....

....

Answer _____ (4)

(b)

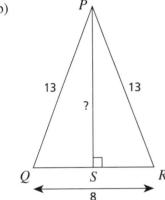

....

....

....

....

....

Answer _____ (3)

*(c)

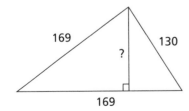

....

....

....

....

....

Answer _____ (6)

14 This is Shirley's garden shed.

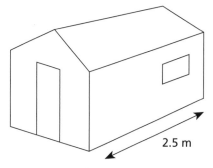

It is 2.5 m long. Here are the plan and elevations of the shed:

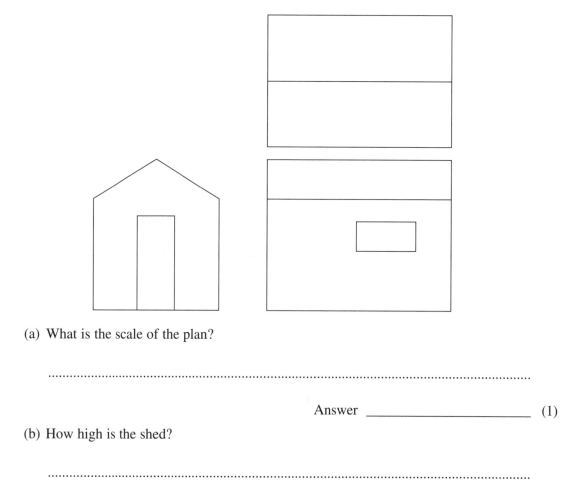

(a) What is the scale of the plan?

....

Answer _____ (1)

(b) How high is the shed?

....

Answer _____ m (1)

(c) Shirley has a pole 3.25 m long. She tries to put it in the shed as shown:

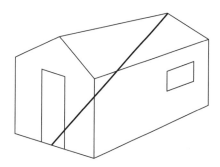

Use calculation to see whether it will fit.

....

.... (3)

(d) Find the length of the longest pole that will fit into the shed in any position.

....

....

....

....

Answer _____ m (5)

15 4 cylindrical rods, each of radius 1 cm are packed into a cylindrical container as shown below. (The centres of the rods are at the corners of a square.)

Calculate the radius of the container.

....

....

....

Answer _____ cm (5)

16 The depth of water in the harbour at St Nazaire is given by the formula

$$D = L + K \sin(29.2t)°$$

where $L - K$ is the depth at low tide
        $L + K$ is the depth at high tide
        t is the time in hours since midnight on 1 July.

(a) At what time is the first high tide on 1 July?

....

....

Answer _____ (2)

(b) At what time is the first low tide on 1 July?

....

....

Answer _____ (2)

(c) Is the depth of water in the harbour more or less at midnight on 2 July than at midnight on 1 July? Show how you decided.

....

....

Answer _____ (2)

(d) Is the tide rising or falling at midnight on 5 July? Show how you decided.

....

....

Answer _____ (3)

17 A party of hikers is walking across open moorland using a compass.

They have been walking on a bearing of 326°. They decide to turn back and retrace their steps.

(a) On what bearing should they walk?

....

Answer _____ (1)

Near the end of the walk there is a steep descent. Lesley decides to check the gradient from the map.

The top has height 293 m and $\frac{1}{2}$ km further on they cross the 150 m contour.

(b) What is the average gradient?

....

....

Answer _____ (2)

18 This solid is made from seven unit cubes:

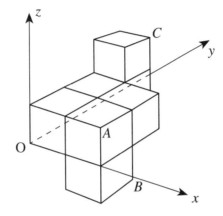

Write down the coordinates of   (a) *A*,   (b) *B*,   (c) *C*.

Answer (a) (__ , __ , __ ,) (b) (__ , __ , __ ,) (c) (__ , __ , __ ,)   (3)

19 Here are some expressions associated with a sphere:

$$\frac{4}{3}\pi r^3, \quad \pi h^2\left(r - \frac{h}{3}\right), \quad 2\pi rk, \quad 2\pi r^2.$$

(*r*, *h*, *k* are all lengths)
Which of these expressions could be areas? Explain.

....

....

....

Answer _____ (2)

20 Two people are pulling ropes attached to a box as shown:

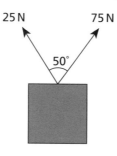

(a) Sketch a vector triangle to show the resultant force.

(2)

*(b) Find the size of the resultant force and the angle it makes with the 25 N force.

....

....

....

Answer _____ N, _____ ° (8)

21 This picture shows a goods van as used on the Welshpool and Llanfair Railway.

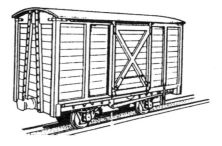

This diagram shows one end.

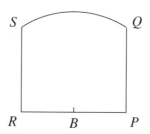

The roof is a circular arc, centre B.
$RP = 2.10$ m, $PQ = 2.33$ m.

(a) Calculate   (i) the length of *BQ*,

....

....

Answer _____ m (2)

(ii) the angle *BQP*,

....

....

Answer _____ ° (3)

(iii) the length of the arc *QS*.

....

....

Answer _____ cm (3)

(b) Calculate the area of the end *RSQP*.

....

....

....

Answer _____ m^2 (4)

Penelope has made a model of the van to a scale $\frac{1}{19}$.

(c) (i) How wide is the model?

....

Answer _____ cm (1)

(ii) What is the area of the end of the model?

....

....

Answer _____ cm^2 (2)

22 The diagram represents the windscreen wiper on a bus.

It is made of three rigid arms, *PA*, *QB* and *AB*. They are loosely jointed at *A* and *B*. *XY* is the wiper blade and is rigidly fixed to *AB* at right angles.

PA = *QB* and *AB* = *PQ*. *P* and *Q* are pivots fixed to the bus and *PQ* is horizontal. The arm *QB* rotates about *Q* and the arm *PA* rotates about *P*.

(a) Explain why *AB* stays horizontal as *QB* rotates.

....

.... (1)

(b) Describe the locus of (i) *B* and (ii) *X*.

B ....

X .... (2)

QB rotates in each direction in turn, stopping when it makes an angle of 40° with the vertical.

(c) Sketch the shape wiped by the blade *XY*.

(2)

*23 The matrix $\begin{pmatrix} 0 & -1 \\ 1 & 0 \end{pmatrix}$ represents the transformation *X*.

(a) (i) Find the image of (5, 2) under *X*.

....

.... (2)

(ii) Find the image of $(-3, 4)$ under X.

....

.... (2)

(iii) Describe the transformation X.

....

.... (2)

(b) What transformation will return these points to their original positions? Write down its matrix.

....

.... (2)

There are two main sections in this attainment target – **processing and interpreting data** and **probability**.

Questions involving the **processing and interpreting of information** may include the drawing of graphs – e.g. histograms and cumulative frequency curves and using these to estimate median and interquartile range, as well as the drawing of bar charts and pie charts. The median and mode, as well as the mean, may, in some questions, have to be calculated.

Example 1: The table shows the heights of 50 eight-year-old boys. Calculate estimates for (a) the mean height and (b) the median height of the boys.

Height (h cm)	Number
$96 \leqslant h < 100$	1
$100 \leqslant h < 104$	3
$104 \leqslant h < 108$	8
$108 \leqslant h < 112$	12
$112 \leqslant h < 116$	13
$116 \leqslant h < 120$	7
$120 \leqslant h < 124$	4
$124 \leqslant h < 128$	2

[describe the dispersion of a set of data, calculate the standard deviation, consider different shapes of histograms with special reference to mean, dispersion and the normal distribution]

* indicates grade
   A* level material

*Example 2:   Find the standard deviation of the heights in Example 1.

Questions may also be set on the interpretation of various types of diagrams *[interpret diagrams such as those used in critical-path analysis or linear programming]*.

Questions concerned with **probability** will extend from straightforward ones such as:

Example 3:   Find the probability of drawing a black ball from a bag containing 10 black balls, 15 red balls and 20 green balls

to more involved ones:

Example 4:   A bag contains 8 red marbles and 6 yellow marbles. Three marbles are taken from the bag at random and not replaced. Find the probability of drawing (a) three red ones, (b) three yellow ones and (c) at least one red marble.

If you need to
revise this
subject more
thoroughly,
see the relevant
topics in the
Letts GCSE
*Mathematics
Study Guide.*

Answers to examples:

1: mean = [98 × 1 + 102 × 3 + ...] ÷ 50 = 112.4 cm,
    median (between 25th and 26th) is just in the interval $112 \leqslant h < 116$
    = 112 cm

*2: 6.20 cm

3: $\dfrac{2}{9}$

4: $\dfrac{2}{13}$, $\dfrac{5}{91}$, $\dfrac{86}{91}$

1 Alfalfa (or lucerne) is a plant used for animal fodder and the extraction of chlorophyll. It can be grown in water.

An experiment was conducted, growing alfalfa in various depths of water. The table shows the results:

Depth of water (cm)	30	45	60	75	90	105	120
Yield of alfalfa (tonnes/hectare)	13.1	14.1	15.6	17.8	20.3	21.5	20.8

(a) Draw a scatter diagram for these data. (2)

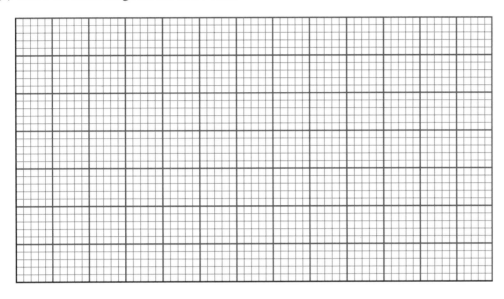

(b) Draw a line of best fit on the diagram. (1)

(c) Estimate the yield for a depth of 100 cm.

Answer _____ tonnes/hectare (1)

(d) Why would you not use your line to estimate the yield at depth 150 cm?

.... (2)

2 The salaries of 8 employees working in a department of a large company are as follows:

£21 000   £23 500   £27 500   £36 000   £19 000   £23 500   £19 000   £19 000

(a) Find the mean, median and mode of their salaries.

....

Mean = £ _____ Median = £ _____ Mode = £ _____ (3)

(b) Which one does not give a good indication of their average salary? Why?

.... (1)

*3 (a) The table below shows the one-stage routes for a bus service in part of a city.

		To			
		A	**B**	**C**	**D**
	A	0	0	1	1
From	**B**	1	0	0	0
	C	0	1	0	1
	D	1	0	1	0

For instance, there one route directly from B to A.
Draw a network to show this information.

(3)

(b) This network diagram shows the one-stage routes in another part of the city.

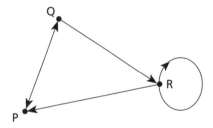

Complete the table for this network.

	P	**Q**	**R**
P			
Q			
R			

(2)

4 The West Albion Garden Society has tested two brands of fertilizer for growing marrows.
Unfortunately the groupings are different and the results difficult to compare.

BRAND A	
Mass in kg	Frequency
Less than 0.5	1
$\geqslant 0.5$ and < 1.0	7
$\geqslant 1.0$ and < 2.5	12
$\geqslant 2.5$ and < 5.0	10
$\geqslant 5.0$ and < 10	3

BRAND B	
Mass in kg	Frequency
Less than 1.0	4
$\geqslant 1.0$ and < 2.0	4
$\geqslant 2.0$ and < 3.0	6
$\geqslant 3.0$ and < 4.0	6
$\geqslant 4.0$ and < 5.0	7
$\geqslant 5.0$ and < 10	3

(a) Draw the histograms.

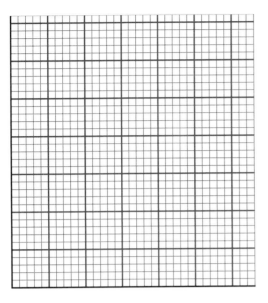
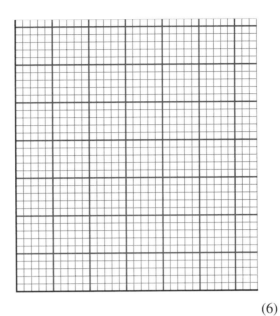

(6)

*(b) Calculate estimates of the mean and standard deviation for each brand.

....

....

Answers

A	Mean:	SD:
B	Mean:	SD:

(5)

(c) Compare the results.

.... (2)

5 A historian is comparing the populations of England and Wales in 1881 and 1951.
   These are the distributions for the male population (in 1000's):

Age	Mid-value	Number of men 1881	Number of men 1951	Cumulative frequency 1881	Cumulative frequency 1951
Under 15		4740	3785		
15 and under 30		3380	4150		
30 and under 45		2250	4639		
45 and under 60		1430	3722		
60 and under 75		710	2232		
75 and over		110	534		

(Take the mid-value of the '75 and over' group to be 82.5, that is everyone is under 90.)

QUESTIONS

(a) (i) Draw the two frequency polygons on the same axes. Label each.

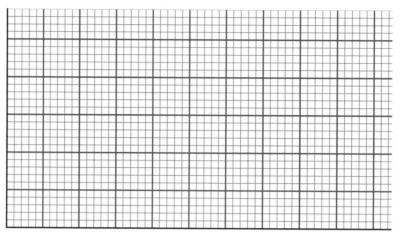

(4)

(ii) Calculate the mean ages in 1881 and 1951.

....

Mean age (1881) _____ (2)

....

Mean age (1951) _____ (2)

(iii) Comment on the differences between the two distributions.

.... (2)

(b) (i) Use the spare columns to write down the cumulative frequencies. (2)

(ii) Draw the cumulative frequency curves on the same axes below. Label each. (4)

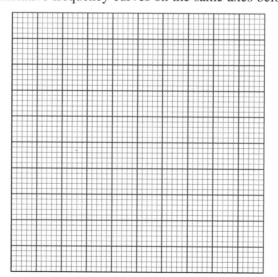

(c) Use the curves to find, for each year,

(i) the median ages,

(ii) the interquartile ranges,

(iii) the percentages of the male populations over 21.

....

....

Answers:

	Median	IQ range	% over 21
1881			
1951			

(6)

(d) Comment on any other differences.

.... (2)

*6 The Podmore family have moved into a new house. They are going to make the garden. Here are the tasks and how long they will take in days:

A	Clear rubbish	5
B	Excavate pond	1
C	Landscape	8
D	Lay lawn	2
E	Paving	10
F	Planning	2
G	Planting	2
H	Pond	1
I	Prepare beds	5
J	Prepare lawn	3

They have drawn this diagram to help them:

```
                                    5
                          I ——————— G
                 8                        \   2
          C ————————<                      \
                          J ——— D           \
                               3   \  2      \
       A \  5                        \        \
  START<                              \        END
       F / 2        E  ——————————————— /
                          10          /
                                     / 1
          B ——— H ——————————————————/
              1
```

(a) Which is the critical path?

....

Answer _____ (1)

(b) How long will it take to complete the garden?

....

Answer _____ (1)

(c) How many people will be needed to complete it in this time? Explain.

....

.... (3)

*7 A builder is planning to build some executive houses and some smaller houses on a $9000 \, m^2$ plot of land. The local council has insisted that:

(i) there must be more smaller houses than executive houses.
(ii) there must be at least 8 executive houses.

(a) Using s for the number of smaller houses and e for the number of executive houses, write down two inequalities to show these conditions.

Answer (a) _____ (2)

The builder knows that he needs $300 \, m^2$ for each smaller house and $500 \, m^2$ for each executive house.

(b) Write down an inequality to show this condition.

Answer (b) _____ (1)

(c) On the graph below show the regions which represent these three conditions, and use your graph to find:

(i) the maximum number of small houses that he can build;

(ii) the maximum number of executive houses that he can build. (5)

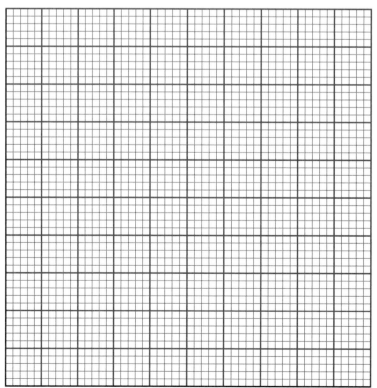

(d) If the selling prices are £65 000 for a small house and £120 000 for an executive house, find the solution which gives the builder the greatest income. Make your method clear.

....

....

....

Answer (d) _____ (2)

8   A card is selected at random from an ordinary pack of 52 playing cards.

(a) What is the probability of selecting either a red king or a red queen?

....

....

Answer (a) _____ (1)

The pack of cards now has all the jacks, queens and kings removed.

(b) What is the probability of drawing a black six from the remaining cards?

....

....

Answer (b) _____ (1)

9   John makes a spinner game for the school fete. When the pointer is spun the probabilities of scoring a colour or a number are given on the table below.

Colour	Probability
white	0.375
purple	0.25
red	0.125
yellow	0.125
blue	0.125

Number	Probability
1	0.25
2	0.25
4	0.5

(a) Find the probability of scoring either a 1 or a 4.

....

Answer (a) _____ (2)

(b) Find the probability of getting a purple or a red.

....

Answer (b) _____ (2)

(c) Why is the probabilty of spinning a 1 or a white not 0.25 + 0.375?

.... (3)

10 Little Amy has two spinners, one with four sides, numbered 1, 2, 3, 4 and the other with six sides numbered 1, 2, 3, 4, 5, 6.

She spins both of them.

(a) List all the possible outcomes.

....

.... (2)

(b) Make a table showing the sum of the two numbers for each outcome.

(2)

(c) What is the probability that

(i) the sum is 5, (ii) the sum is odd?

....

Answers: (i) _____ (ii) _____ (2)

Amy's elder brother Richard thinks that the probability of the sum being either 5 or an odd number can be found by adding the two previous answers.

(d) Explain why he is wrong.

.... (1)

(e) How can you work out the probability that the sum is even without using the table?

.... (1)

11 The table shows the number of 999 calls received in one area:

Police	83
Ambulance	92
Fire	16
Coastguard	4

Based on these data, what is the probability that the next call received is for

(a) an ambulance,　　(b) fire or the coastguard?

....

....

Answers: (a) _____ (b) _____ (3)

12 Malcolm is playing a game with three ordinary dice, faces numbered 1, 2, 3, 4, 5, 6.
He throws each in turn. He wins the game if any one shows a six.

(a) (i)　Complete the tree diagram.

$\frac{1}{6}$ — Six

Not a six

Six

Not a six

Six

Not a six

(2)

(ii)　What is the probability that he wins with the second throw?

....

Answer _____ (2)

(iii) What is the probability that he wins?

....

....

Answer _____ (3)

Veronica is playing another game with six cards numbered 1, 2, 3, 4, 5, 6. She takes a card at random and does not replace it. If it is a six she wins. If not, she draws another card, again not replacing it. If it is a six she wins. If not, a third card is drawn. If it is a six she wins.

(b) (i) Complete the tree diagram.

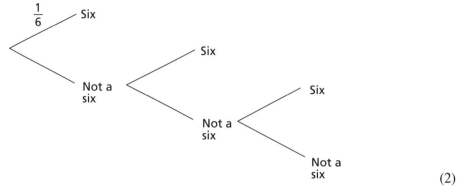

(2)

(ii) What is the probability that she wins with the second draw?

....

Answer _____ (2)

(iii) What is the probability that she wins?

....

....

Answer _____ (3)

(iv) Explain how you could have found the answer to (iii) another way.

.... (1)

*13 How many times must you toss a fair coin for the probability of getting at least one head to be more than 0.95?

....

....

Answer _____ (5)

1 NUMBER

Question	Answer	Mark
1	$733.60 - 40 \times 7.30 = 441.60$	1
	$441.60 \div 36.80 = 12$	1

Examiner's tip It is not necessary to write down the intermediate step but it is a good idea to do so in case you make an error in the second step.

2	$\dfrac{4.7 - 3.6}{3.6} \times 100$	1
	$= 30.55555555... = 30.6\%$	1

Examiner's tip Most calculators require you to key = before ÷ 3.6. It is better to round your answer than leave a string of decimals. You could argue for the answer to be given as 31 as the data was given to two significant figures.

3	$\dfrac{7000 \times 400}{60\,000\,000} \times 100$	1
	$= 4.7\%$ or 5%	1

Examiner's tip The data given is already approximate so no rounding is needed until the final answer. This has been given to 1 or 2 significant figures, although only one significant figure is justified by 1 significant figure data.

4	$\dfrac{12\,800 - 12\,400}{12\,800} \times 100$	1
	$= 3.125\%$	1

Examiner's tip In this question the amount was reduced but it is still the starting value that appears under the fraction.

5	I increased by 10% means it is multiplied by 1.10	1
	R increased by 20% means it is multiplied by 1.20	1
	$V = IR$ is multiplied by $1.1 \times 1.2 = 1.32$	1
	V is increased by 32%	1

Examiner's tip Using multipliers is the easiest way to tackle this sort of problem.

Question	Answer	Mark
6 (a)	5×10^9	1
(b)	$\dfrac{4 \times 10^{11}}{5 \times 10^9}$	1
	$= 8 \times 10$	1

7	$P = \sqrt{\dfrac{4.6 \times 10^6}{2.8 \times 10^2}} = 128.173\,9889$	1
	$= 1.28 \times 10^2 \text{ or } 1.3 \times 10^2$	1

Examiner's tip Notice that there is a mark for getting the calculation right even if it is not in standard form. Your calculator may not show as many digits as this.

8 (a) (i) 0.021 358 613	(ii) 0.0214 or 0.021	2+1

Examiner's tip This is firstly a test to see if you can use your calculator correctly. A common error is to multiply by 6.81 rather than divide by it. The decision about the answer to (ii), in the absence of other information, is based on the number of figures in each item. In this case two are given to 3 significant figures and it is reasonable to keep to this, or one less, in your answer.

(b)	3.9024	2

Examiner's tip This again is to test your ability to use the calculator. It is more efficient to use brackets or the memory than write down an intermediate answer. In all calculator questions it is a good idea to check your answer, either by doing it again, preferably a different way, or by making an estimate to see if your answer is about right.

9 (a)	$\dfrac{1764 - 1575}{1575} \times 100$	1
	$= 12\%$	1
(b)	Interest over 12 months nearly £200.	1
	Interest over 24 months nearly £400, about twice as much.	1

Examiner's tip A useful guide in this sort of question is to round the numbers so that you can work it out in your head. In this case you might have preferred to use more accurate estimates, such as £190 and £380. There is no need to work out the rate of interest. You can, of course, check it on your calculator, unless the question is asked in a section in which calculators are not permitted.

Question	Answer	Mark
10 (a)	65	1
(b)	67.5, 62.5	1+1
(c)	No — the upper bound on the balance is 62.5 which is less than the lower bound on the scales.	1
	The scales and the electronic scales could both be right since 65 < 67.5.	1

| **11** | $s = \dfrac{25.0^2 - 50.0^2}{2 \times {}^-9.8}$ | 2 |
| | $= 95.7$ or 96 $\quad$ (95.663 265 31) | 1 |

Examiner's tip Care needs to be taken with the negative sign when you divide by -9.8, most calculators requiring you to key $\pm$ after entering 9.8.

12 (a)	$22 \sin 70° = 20.67$, $\quad 28 \sin 48° = 20.81$	2+1
	Perpendicular distance between longest sides is nearly the same at each end.	1
	Longest sides are nearly parallel, so quadrilateral is roughly a trapezium.	1

Examiner's tip The first part of this question requires you to use knowledge from a different attainment target but this is to enable you to tackle the next part. If you did not spot how to do this, come back to it again after practice in a later section.

*(b)	Area of largest possible trapezium must be found using upper bounds of lengths.	1
	Maximum area $= \frac{1}{2} \times 21.5 \times (32.5 + 58.5)$	2
	$= 978.25$	1
	Yes, this is less than 1000.	1

Examiner's tip This could have been treated in a more complicated way by using the maximum possible distance between the 'parallel' sides, i.e. $28.5 \sin 48.5°$, which is 21.3 and $22.5 \sin 70°$, which is 21.2, both smaller than 21.5 which had been taken as the upper bound of 21. The result would clearly have been smaller.
   In some problems it may be necessary to take a lower bound, even though the maximum value of the expression is required, for example where division is involved.

13	31/12/90: Amount owing $= 650 \times 1.06 - 243 = £446$	1
	31/12/91: Amount owing $= 446 \times 1.06 - 243 = £229.76$	1
	31/12/92: Amount owing $= 229.76 \times 1.06 - 243 = £0.55$	1

Examiner's tip The final answer has been written correct to the nearest penny.

Question	Answer	Mark

*14 Maximum average speed $= \dfrac{400.5}{49.35}$ **2**

$= 8.1155\ldots$ or 8.11 **1**

> **Examiner's tip** This is an example where the upper bound of the speed is obtained using the upper bound of the distance with the lower bound of the time. It is not sensible to round up since this would be above the upper bound.

15 (a) $3.142 = \dfrac{3142}{1000}$ which is rational   **1**

(b) $1.\dot{6} = 1\frac{2}{3}$ which is rational   **1**

(c) $\left(\sqrt{3}\right)^3 = 3\sqrt{3}$ which is irrational   **1**

(d) $(1 + \sqrt{3})(1 - \sqrt{3}) = 1 + \sqrt{3} - \sqrt{3} - 3$ **1**

$= {}^{-}2$ which is rational   **1**

(e) $\dfrac{\left(1 + \sqrt{3}\right)}{\left(1 - \sqrt{3}\right)} = \dfrac{\left(1 + \sqrt{3}\right)\left(1 + \sqrt{3}\right)}{\left(1 - \sqrt{3}\right)\left(1 + \sqrt{3}\right)} = \dfrac{1 + 2\sqrt{3} + 3}{{}^{-}2}$ **2**

$= {}^{-}2 - \sqrt{3}$ irrational   **1**

> **Examiner's tip** To show that a number is rational it is necessary to show that it can be written as a fraction using whole numbers. In this case an approach to part (e) was suggested by the work in part (d).

2 ALGEBRA

Question	Answer	Mark

1 (a) $(6 \times 7) + 4$ **1**

(b) $(8 \times 9) + 6$ **1**

(c) $(n + 2)(n + 3) + n$ **1**

$n^2 + 2n + 3n + 6 + n$ **1**

$n^2 + 6n + 6$ **1**

> **Examiner's tip** 'Simplify your answer' means that you are expected to collect like terms, in this case that means adding together all the n terms.

2 (a) (i)   38, 51   **1**

(ii)   The differences between terms are successive odd numbers, so the next term will be 51 + the next odd number, 15.   **1**

Question	Answer	Mark

(b)　(i)　n^2 — **1**

(ii)　Each term is 2 more than the term in the sequence in (b)(i). — **1**
　　　$n^2 + 2$ — **1**

> **Examiner's tip** You can find this nth term using the differences noted in part (a) but the question has been arranged to help you spot the connection between the sequence and the more familiar square numbers.

3　(a)　Next term will be the mean of the previous two terms. — **1**

*　(b)　Next three terms are $1\frac{11}{16}$, $1\frac{21}{32}$, $1\frac{43}{64}$, or on the calculator 1.6875,

　　　1.656 25, 1.671 85 — **1**
　　　Two more terms: 1.664 0625, 1.667 956 25 — **1+1**
　　　Limit appears to be $1\frac{2}{3}$. — **1**

> **Examiner's tip** You may prefer to use the differences between successive terms, $^+1$, $^-\frac{1}{2}$, $^-\frac{1}{4}$, $^-\frac{1}{8}$, etc.

4　(a)　$6x^2 + 21x - 12x - 42$ — **1**
　　　$6x^2 + 9x - 42$ — **1**

> **Examiner's tip** This could be written as $3(2x^2 + 3x - 14)$.

(b)　(i)　$(x + 3)(x - 2)$ — **2**

> **Examiner's tip** The '$+x$' in the expression means that it will be '$+3$' and '-2' in the brackets.

(ii)　$x = {}^-3$ or $x = 2$ — **1+1**

5　(a)　$21 - 3x = 4x$　　　(adding 10 to both sides) — **1**
　　　$21 = 7x$　　　(adding $3x$ to both sides) — **1**
　　　$x = 3$　　　(dividing both sides by 7) — **1**

(b)　$x = 2$　　$x^3 = 8$　　(reasonably close trial) — **1**
　　　　1.9　　　　6.859
　　　　1.95　　　7.4148…
　　　　1.92　　　7.0778…　　(just too big) — **1**
　　　　1.91　　　6.9678…　　(just too small) — **1**
　　　　1.915　　7.0227…
　　　1.915 is too big so 1.91 is correct to 2 decimal places. — **1**

> **Examiner's tip** Since the value when $x = 1.92$ is much further from 7 than the value when $x = 1.91$, it is sufficient to give this as your reason for choosing 1.91.

Question	Answer	Mark
6 (a)	The lengths of the three sides are x, x and $22 - 2x$, since the total length of netting is 22 m.	
	Area $= x(22 - 2x) = 60$	1
	$\qquad 22x - 2x^2 = 60 \qquad$ (expanding brackets)	
	$\qquad 11x - x^2 = 30 \qquad$ (dividing by 2)	1
	$\qquad -x^2 + 11x - 30 = 0 \qquad$ (subtracting 30 from each side)	
	$\qquad x^2 - 11x + 30 = 0 \qquad$ (multiplying each side by $^-1$)	1
* (b)	$(x - 5)(x - 6) = 0$	1
	$x - 5 = 0$ or $x - 6 = 0$	1
	$x = 5$ or 6	1

Examiner's tip Since the left-hand side of this equation did factorize, this is the easiest way to solve it. However, the same result would have been achieved by using the quadratic formula or completing the square.

Question	Answer	Mark
(c)	If $x = 5$ the run measures 5 by 12	1
	If $x = 6$ the run measures 6 by 10	1

Examiner's tip Both solutions work in this practical problem. This is not always the case.

Question	Answer	Mark
7 (a)	$3n - 4 < 17$	1
(b)	$3n < 17 + 4$	1
	$n < 7$	1

Examiner's tip Although solving this inequality looks much the same as solving the equation $3n - 4 = 18$, it is important to keep the inequality sign the right way round. In some cases this will not be so obvious.

Question	Answer	Mark
8	$\begin{array}{ll} x = 4 & x^2 - x = 12 \\ \quad 3.5 & \qquad 8.75 \\ \quad 3.8 & \qquad 10.64 \end{array}$	1
	$\begin{array}{ll} \quad 3.85 & \qquad 10.9725 \end{array}$	1
	$\begin{array}{ll} \quad 3.86 & \qquad 11.0396 \end{array}$	1
	$\begin{array}{ll} \quad 3.855 & \qquad 11.006\,025 \end{array}$	
	Since the last value is too big, the solution is 3.85	1

Examiner's tip You must show the results of your trials to convince the examiner that you are using the method. The first mark is for a sensible trial, that is one quite close to the result. The next two are for finding numbers above and below the result and the last for showing how you decided. It is sometimes obvious which is nearer but in this case they gave values differing by almost the same amount from 11.

Question	Answer	Mark

9

$2x + 3y = 17$ ....(i)
$3x − 2y = 6$..................(ii)   number the equations for identification
(i) times 3 gives $6x + 9y = 51$ ....(iii)
(ii) times 2 gives $6x − 4y = 12$ ....(iv)
subtract: $13y = 39$ **1**
therefore $y = 3$ **1**
substitute in (i) gives: $2x + 9 = 17$ **1**
$2x = 8$
$x = 4$ **1**

10

$s = 10 \times 11 \times 21 \div 6$ **1**
$= 385$ **1**

11 (a)

$Q = 3600 \times 12 \times 2 \div 55$ **1**
$= 1570(.909...)$ **1**

(b)

$1000 = 3600 \times 15 \times N \div 120$ **1**
$N = 1000 \times 120 \div 3600 \div 15$ **1**
$= 2.2...$, i.e. 3 lanes.   **1**

12

$F = 2C$ **1**
$C = \frac{5}{9}(2C − 32)$ (substituting for F)   **1**
$9C = 10C − 160$ (multiplying by 9 and expanding the bracket)   **1**
$−C = −160$ (subtracting $10C$ from both sides)
$C = 160$ **1**

Question	Answer	Mark
13	Mean $= (30 + 40 + x + 50 + 80) \div 5 = 40 + \dfrac{x}{5}$	1
	Median $= x$	1
	$40 + \dfrac{x}{5} = x$	1
	$\dfrac{4}{5}x = 40$ (subtracting $\dfrac{x}{5}$ from both sides)	1
	$x = 50$ (multiplying by 5 and dividing by 4)	1

Examiner's tip   You can be asked to form an equation before solving it.

Question	Answer	Mark
14 (a)	$3d + 7w = 53.4$	1
	$d + 10w = 50$	1
(b)	$3d + 30w = 150$ (multiplying second equation by 3)	1
	$3d + 7w = 53.4$ (first equation)	
	$23w = 96.6$ (subtracting the equations)	1
	$w = 4.2$ (dividing by 23)	1
	$d = 50 - 10 \times 4.2 = 8$ (substituting in second equation)	1

Question	Answer	Mark
15	0, 1, 2, 3	2

Examiner's tip   Notice that $^-1$ is not included as the numbers must be greater than it. However 3 is included as that inequality sign includes 'equals'.

16 (a)

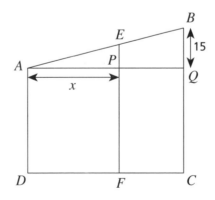

APE and *AQB* are similar triangles so

$\dfrac{PE}{QB} = \dfrac{AP}{AQ}$	(ratios of corresponding sides)	1
$PE = x \times 15 \div 60 = \dfrac{1}{4}x$	(substituting)	1
$EF = FP + PE = 25 + \dfrac{1}{4}x$		1

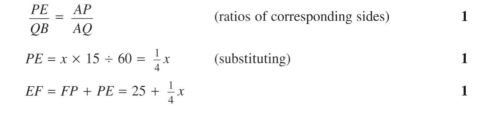

Question	Answer	Mark
(b)	Area of $AEFD = \frac{1}{2}x\,(AD + EF) = \frac{1}{2}x\,(25 + 25 + \frac{1}{4}x)$	1
	Area of $AEFD = \frac{1}{2}$ area $ABCD = \frac{1}{4} \times 60 \times (25 + 40)$	1
	$25x + \frac{1}{8}x^2 = 975$ (simplifying and putting areas equal)	1
	$x^2 + 200x - 7800 = 0$ (multiply by 8 and rearrange)	

Question	Answer		Mark
(c)	$x = 30$	$x^2 + 200x - 7800 = -900$	
	35	425	1
	33	-111	
	33.5	22.25	
	33.4	-4.44	1
	33.4 is closer		1

Examiner's tip As an alternative, if you know the method, you could use the quadratic formula or 'completing the square'. This quadratic expression did not factorize and there was a clue to this in the question – the answer was asked to the nearest 0.1 m.

Question	Answer	Mark
(d)	It is just to the right of halfway and DF will be wider than FC since AD is shorter than BC.	1

Question	Answer	Mark
17	$20 = \sqrt{\dfrac{2 \times 3950 \times h}{5280}}$	1
	$h = \dfrac{20^2 \times 5280}{2 \times 3950}$	1
	$= 267(.34...)$	1

Examiner's tip You could also rearrange the formula before substituting. The formula would be
$$h = \frac{5280 D^2}{2r}$$

Question	Answer	Mark
18	$PV = k$ (multiplying both sides by V)	1
	$V = \dfrac{k}{P}$ (dividing both sides by P)	1

Examiner's tip It is safer to do this in two simple steps.

Question	Answer	Mark
19	(a) $2x \leqslant 15$ (adding 7 to both sides)	
	$\quad\;\; x \leqslant 7\frac{1}{2}$ (dividing both sides by 2)	1
	(b) $^-x > ^-1$ (subtracting 3 from both sides)	
	$\quad\;\; x < 1$ (dividing both sides by $^-1$ and changing sign)	1

Question	Answer	Mark

It is important to notice that if you change the signs of the two sides of an inequality, in this case from negative to positive, it is necessary to change the inequality sign also. For example, $7 > 4$ but $^-7 < ^-4$.

You can do it another way:

$3 > 2 + x$ (adding x to both sides)
$1 > x$ (subtracting 2 from both sides)
$x < 1$ (writing from right to left)

(c) $x^2 < 4$ (subtracting 4 from both sides)
If $x > 0$, $x < 2$ (taking positive square root)   **1**
If $x < 0$, $x > ^-2$ (taking negative square root and therefore changing inequality sign)   **1**

These two inequalities can be combined as $^-2 < x < 2$.

20   Let the lengths of the sides of the rectangle be x and y.
$xy = 6$ (area of rectangle)   **1**

$\sqrt{x^2 + y^2} = \sqrt{13}$ or $x^2 + y^2 = 13$ (using Pythagoras)   **1**

$x^2 + \dfrac{36}{x^2} = 13$ (substituting for y from first equation)   **1**

$x^4 - 13x^2 + 36 = 0$ (multiplying each side by x^2 and rearranging)   **1**

$(x^2 - 9)(x^2 - 4) = 0$ (factorizing)   **1**

$x^2 = 9$ or 4, $x = 3$ or 2 **1**

Although it looks as though this is an equation in x^4 it is only a quadratic in x^2, from the practical point of view. Notice that it is not necessary to consider the negative solutions since the problem was about actual lengths.

21 (a)   Area $= y^2 - 4 \times \frac{1}{2}x^2$ **1**
         $= y^2 - 2x^2$ **1**

(b) $x^2 + x^2 = 14^2$ (applying Pythagoras to any corner triangle)   **1**
         $2x^2 = 196$
         $x^2 = 98$
         $x = 9.899...$ **1**

Although not a sensible degree of accuracy for a practical problem, keep all the figures on your calculator for the next calculations.

(c) $y = 14 + 2x = 33.798...$ **1**

     Area $= 33.798^2 - 2 \times 9.899^2$ **1**
         $= 946 \text{ cm}^2$ **1**

Question	Answer	Mark

22 (a)   If it were linear the increases would be in proportion:
Speed goes up in steps of 20 but distance goes up 100 then 140.   **1**

(b)   If $d \propto s^2$, then $\left(\dfrac{30}{50}\right)^2 (= 0.36)$ should equal $\left(\dfrac{75}{175}\right) (= 0.42...)$ **1**

(c) $75 = 30t + 900k$
$175 = 50t + 2500k$ **1**
$375 = 150t + 4500k$ (multiplying first by 5)
$525 = 150t + 7500k$ (multiplying second by 3)   **1**
$150 = 3000k$ (subtracting)   **1**
$k = 0.05$ **1**
$t = (75 - 900 \times 0.05) \div 30 = 1$ **1**

23 (a) $x^{3/2}$ **1**

(b) x^{-2} **1**

(c) $x^6 y^4$ **1**

24 (a) and (b)

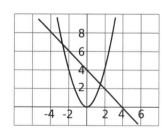

Straight line **1**
Curve **2**

(c)   (i)   1.6, $^-2.6$ **1+1**

Question	Answer		Mark
(ii)	$x = 1.6$	$x^2 + x - 4 =$ 0.16	
	1.55	-0.0475	
	1.57	0.0349	
	1.56	-0.0064	1
	1.56 is closer		1
	-2.6	0.16	
	-2.5	-0.25	
	-2.57	0.0349	
	-2.56	-0.0064	1
	-2.56 is closer		1

Examiner's tip You should not need many trials as the starting point was quite accurate.

---

25 (a) and (b)

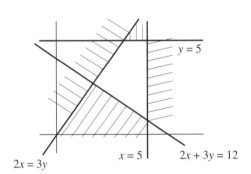

4

Examiner's tip If you shade the regions which are **not** included it will be easier to look for possible solution points, should they be asked for.

26

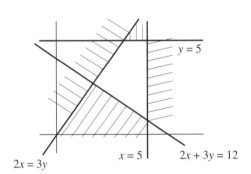

	Mark
	1
	1+1
	1

27

A: Cycling at constant speed	1
B: Slowing down (going uphill)	1
C: Accelerating (going downhill)	1
D: Maximum speed (bottom of hill)	1

Question	Answer	Mark

> **Examiner's tip** Do not be deceived into thinking that when the graph goes up it is a hill! It actually means the cyclist is going faster, so it is more likely to be down a hill.

28 (a)   Tangent drawn at $t = 4$ 1
                   $42 \div 8 = 5.25$ 1
                   Units m/s^2 1

> **Examiner's tip** Try to draw the tangent so that it touches at time $t = 4$. Take the measurements to calculate the gradient as large as the diagram will allow.

* (b)   Attempt at area under curve up to 10 seconds   1

$$\frac{1}{2}(0 + 55) + 12 + 23 + 31 + 37 + 42 + 46 + 50 + 52 + 54$$

(trapezium rule using 10 strips)   2

$= 374.5$ or $370\,$m   1

> **Examiner's tip** You could also have obtained this answer by counting squares.

*29

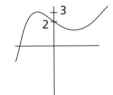  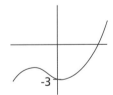 

                                                    4
                                       (one mark each)

> **Examiner's tip** Make sure you label any points on the axes of the sketches to show how the position has changed.

3 SHAPE AND SPACE

Question	Answer	Mark

1   Area of rhombus is half area of rectangle   1
               Area $= \frac{1}{2} \times 1.6 \times 0.8$ 1
                       $= 0.64$ 1

Question	Answer	Mark

An alternative method is to divide the rhombus into four right-angled triangles, using the diagonals.

2 (a)   Radius $= \frac{1}{2} \times (4 + 6)$ **1**

                      $= 5$ **1**

     (b)   Area $= \pi \times 2^2 + \pi \times 3^2$ **2**

                    $= 40.8$ **1**

You will have to remember the formula for the area of a circle, πr^2

3   Area of rectangle $= 6 \times 12$ **1**

                     $= 72$ **1**

           Area of circles $= 2 \times \pi \times 3^2$ **1**

                     $= 56.5...$ **1**

           Area left $= 72 - 56.5... = 15.45$ or 15.5 **1**

You do not need to write down the intermediate answers but it is wise to show how you did the calculation in case you make an error. The marks for your method could still be given.

4   The pool is a prism whose cross section is a trapezium.   **1**

           Area of cross section $= \frac{1}{2} \times 25 \times (2 + 4)$ **1**

                         $= 75$ **1**

           Volume $= 15 \times 75 = 1125$ **1**

The top edge of the pool is horizontal and the sides vertical, so the diagram shows the cross section:

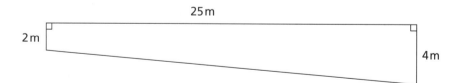

5   Scale factor for large ball from small ball $= 3$

           Volume scale factor $= 3^3$ **1**

           27 small balls   **1**

Question	Answer	Mark

6

Area of complete rectangle $= 3r \times 2r$ **1**

$\qquad\qquad\qquad\qquad = 6r^2$ **1**

Area of semicircle removed $= \frac{1}{2}\pi r^2$ Area required $= 6r^2 - \frac{1}{2}\pi r^2$ **1+1**

---

7 (a)

$\dfrac{36}{30} = \dfrac{36 - h}{10}$ **1**

$12 = 36 - h \qquad h = 24$ **1+1**

(b)   Slant height of complete cone $= \sqrt{36^2 + 15^2}$ **1**

$\qquad\qquad\qquad\qquad\qquad\qquad = 39$ **1**

Slant height of small cone $= \frac{1}{3} \times 39 = 13$ **1**

Surface area of complete cone $= \pi \times 15 \times 39$ **1**

Surface area of small cone $= \pi \times 5 \times 13$ **1**

Surface area of shade $= 585\pi - 65\pi = 520\pi = 1634\,\text{cm}^2$ **1**

8

Circumference of two inner semicircles $= 400 - 2 \times 90 = 220$ **1**

Radius of inner semicircles $= 220 \div 2\pi = 35.014...$ **1**

Radius of outer semicircles $= 8 + 35.014... = 43.014...$ **1**

Circumference of two outer semicircles $= 2 \times \pi \times 43.014 = 270$ **1**

Extra distance $= 270 - 220 = 50$ **1**

---

9 (a)

Volume $= \pi \times 1.5^2 \times 14.5$ **1**

$\qquad\quad = 102.4944...$ **1**

(b)   Volume of toothpaste 'cylinder' $= \pi \times 3.5^2 \times 15\,\text{mm}^3$ **1**

$1\,\text{cm}^3 = 1000\,\text{mm}^3$ **1**

Question	Answer	Mark

$$\text{Number of times} = \frac{\pi \times 1.5^2 \times 14.5 \times 1000}{\pi \times 3.5^2 \times 15}$$

1

$$= 177$$

1

Examiner's tip Don't forget the change of units in part (b). It would not be reasonable to round up the final answer as part of a 'cylinder' is not enough to clean my teeth. In fact the situation is actually more approximate, since toothpaste tubes are not cylinders, but the wording of the question tells you to take it as a cylinder.

10 (a) $\qquad 135 \times \dfrac{110}{90}$

1

$$= 165$$

1

(b) $\qquad$ Area scale factor = (linear scale factor)^2

1

$$\text{Cost} = 7 \times \left(\frac{110}{90}\right)^2$$

1

$$= 10.456...$$

1

Examiner's tip The answer to part (b) could be 10p or 11p, depending on economics! You must make sure you use the area scale factor. It was made clear in the question by stating that the price was proportional to the area.

11 (a) $\qquad ? = \sqrt{14^2 + 8^2}$

2

$$= 16.12...$$

1

Examiner's tip This is the easiest case when using Pythagoras.

(b) $\qquad ? = \sqrt{7^2 - 6^2}$

2

$$= 3.6055...$$

1

Examiner's tip This is the rearranged form, deriving from $7^2 = 6^2 + ?^2$. This question is not set in a practical context so the number of digits in your answer is not important, so long as there are enough to show you have done it correctly, e.g., 16.1 and 3.61 would be perfectly acceptable.

12 (a) $\qquad 5.50 \sin 70° = 5.168...$

2

$$= 5.17$$

1

(b) $\qquad 5.50 \cos 70° = 1.881...$

2

$$= 1.88$$

1

Question	Answer	Mark

(c) $1.8 \tan 67°$ **2**
       $= 4.24$ **1**

13 (a) $CD = 4$ **1**
       $? = 4 \tan 73°$ **2**
        $= 13.08$ **1**

  (b) $? = \sqrt{13^2 - 4^2}$ **2**
        $= 12.37$ **1**

 * (c)   Cosine rule: $130^2 = 169^2 + 169^2 - 2 \times 169 \times 169 \cos x$ **2**
       $x = 45.239\ldots$ **2**
       $? = 169 \sin x$ **1**
        $= 120$ **1**

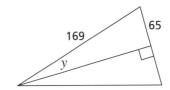
14 (a)   1 to 50   **1**

  (b)   2.0   **1**

  (c) $2.5^2 + 2^2$ **1**
       $= 10.25$ **1**

       $\sqrt{10.25} = 3.20\ldots$ The pole is too long   **1**

  (d)   Width of shed $= 1.75\,\text{m}$
      Two longer positions:

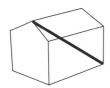

      $\sqrt{2^2 + 2.5^2 + 0.875^2}$ **2**
      $= 3.3189\ldots$ **1**

Question	Answer	Mark

Height at side $= 1.5\,\text{m}$

$$\sqrt{1.5^2 + 1.75^2 + 2.5^2} = 3.400\ldots$$ | 1

This is the longest. | 1

> **Examiner's tip** These solutions use the three-dimensional form of Pythagoras. You may prefer to build this up using the length of the diagonal of the base, or half the base of the shed. Which position gives the longest will depend on the relative dimensions of the shed.

---

15 Square joining centres has side $2\,\text{cm}$ | 1

Diagonal of square $= \sqrt{2^2 + 2^2}$ | 1

$= 2.828\ldots$ | 1

Radius of container = small radius + half diagonal of square | 1

$= 2.414 = 2.41$ | 1

> **Examiner's tip** You may find it helpful to draw your own diagram.

---

16 (a) First high tide when $\sin(29.2t)^\circ = 1$, i.e. when $29.2t = 90$ | 1

$t = 3.082\ldots$ hours: Time is 3.05 am (to nearest minute) | 1

> **Examiner's tip** Don't forget that there are 60 minutes in an hour, not 100!

(b) First low tide when $\sin(29.2t)^\circ = -1$, i.e. when $29.2t = 270$ | 1

$t = 9.246\ldots$ hours: Time is 9.15 am (to nearest minute) | 1

(c) $t = 24$, depth $= L + K\sin(700.8)^\circ = L + (-0.3288\ldots)K$ | 1

The water level is lower on 2 July. | 1

> **Examiner's tip** Most calculators will find the sine automatically.

(d) $t = 96$, depth $= L + K\sin(2803.2)^\circ = L + (-0.9735\ldots)K$ | 1

$t = 96.1$, depth $= L + K\sin(2806.12)^\circ = L + (-0.9606\ldots)K$ | 1

This is higher so the tide is rising. | 1

> **Examiner's tip** Care is needed with the last part since it is not far from low tide. A small difference in time, before or after, is required.

Question	Answer	Mark
17 (a)	$146°$	1

Examiner's tip If in doubt, sketch a diagram.

(b)	Average gradient $= \dfrac{293 - 150}{500}$	1
	$= 0.286$	1

Examiner's tip Don't forget to make the units the same.

18 (a)	$(2, 0, 1)$	1
(b)	$(2, 1, \,^{-}1)$	1
(c)	$(1, 3, 2)$	1

Examiner's tip Count the number of units parallel to the axis in each case.

19	$2\pi rk$, $2\pi r^2$. These could both be areas as they involve length $\times$ length.	1
	The others involve length $\times$ length $\times$ length and could be volumes.	1

20 (a)

75

130°

25

$\qquad$ 2

Examiner's tip It is worth marking the lengths and the angle since you will need them in the next part.

* (b)	Using cosine rule: $(\text{resultant})^2 = 25^2 + 75^2 - 2 \times 25 \times 75 \times \cos 130°$	2
	resultant $= 93.1$	2
	Using sine rule: $\dfrac{93.06\ldots}{\sin 130°} = \dfrac{75}{\sin x}$	2
	$x = 38.1°$	2

Examiner's tip Write down the expressions you are going to evaluate in case you make an error.

Question	Answer	Mark
21 (a) (i)	$BQ = \sqrt{1.05^2 + 2.33^2}$	1
	$= 2.56$	1
(ii)	Angle $BQP = \arctan \dfrac{1.05}{2.33}$	2
	$= 24.26°$	1
(iii)	Arc $QS = \dfrac{2 \times 24.26}{360}$ of full circle radius 2.56 m	1
	$= \dfrac{2 \times 24.26}{360} \times 2 \times \pi \times 2.56$	1
	$= 2.17$ m	1
(b)	Area of end is sector SBQ + triangle SRB + triangle QBP	1
	$= \dfrac{2 \times 24.26}{360} \times \pi \times 2.56^2 + 1.05 \times 2.33$	2
	$= 5.22$	1

> **Examiner's tip** The multiplier for the sector as a fraction of the whole circle is the same for area as arc length. The two triangles in part (b) are the same size and together make a rectangle.

(c) (i)	$2.1 \times \dfrac{1}{19} = 0.1105$ m or 11.05 cm	1
(ii)	$5.22 \times \left(\dfrac{1}{19}\right)^2$	1
	$= 0.01446$ m^2 or 144.6 cm^2	1

> **Examiner's tip** Remember the area scale factor is squared and there are 10 000 cm^2 in 1 m^2.

22 (a)	$ABQP$ is a parallelogram so AB remains parallel to PQ, which is horizontal	1
(b) (i)	B moves on an arc of a circle radius QB	1
(ii)	X moves on an arc of equal size distance XB above B	1
(c)		2

Question	Answer	Mark
*23(a) (i)	($^-$2, 5)	2
(ii)	($^-$4, 3)	2
(iii)	rotation of 90° anticlockwise about the origin	2
(b)	$\begin{pmatrix} 0 & 1 \\ ^-1 & 0 \end{pmatrix}$	2

4 HANDLING DATA

Question	Answer	Mark

1 (a) and (b)

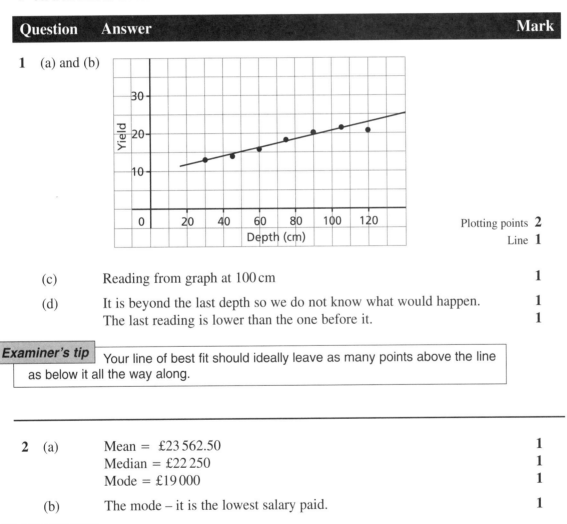

Plotting points **2**
Line **1**

(c)   Reading from graph at 100 cm   **1**

(d)   It is beyond the last depth so we do not know what would happen.   **1**
           The last reading is lower than the one before it.   **1**

Examiner's tip   Your line of best fit should ideally leave as many points above the line as below it all the way along.

2 (a)   Mean = £23 562.50   **1**
           Median = £22 250   **1**
           Mode = £19 000   **1**

(b)   The mode – it is the lowest salary paid.   **1**

Examiner's tip   The median is halfway between the two middle values when they are ranked.

Question	Answer	Mark

3 (a)

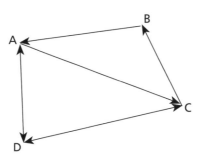

3

(b)

	P	Q	R
P	0	1	0
Q	1	0	1
R	1	0	1

2

Examiner's tip   The arrows show that some routes are one way and some two way.

---

4 (a)

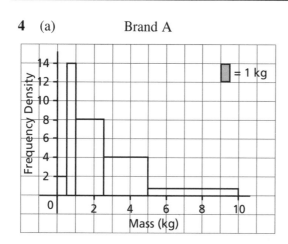

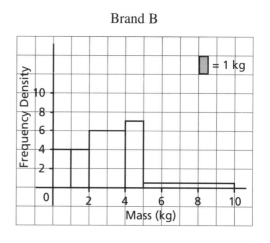

3+3
(1 mark deducted
for each mistake)

Examiner's tip   The sizes of the classes vary in these distributions so the heights of
the columns must be adjusted to make the area of the columns equal the frequency
in each class. The axis up the page is Frequency Density. You must decide on a
unit area.

* (b)   Brand A mid-points: 0.25, 0.75, 1.75, 3.75, 7.5
Brand B mid-points: 0.5, 1.5, 2.5, 3.5, 4.5, 7.5

1

A	Mean: 2.62	SD: 1.93	**1+1**
B	Mean: 3.27	SD: 1.93	**1+1**

Question	Answer	Mark
(c)	Higher mean (better yield on average) from Brand B	1
	Same spread (same degree of variation from the mean)	1

 Examiner's tip A calculator with statistics makes these calculations much simpler and you would probably only have to do one in an examination.

5 (a) (i)

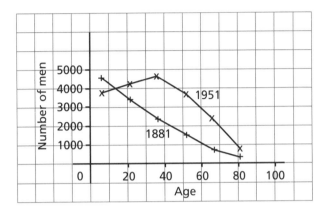

4
(1 mark deducted
for each mistake)

(ii) Mean (1881) = (7.5 × 4740 + 22.5 × 3380 + etc.) ÷ 12 620   1
= 26.0 years   1

Mean (1951) = (7.5 × 3785 + etc.) ÷ 19 062   1
= 36.0 years   1

Examiner's tip If your calculator will do statistics, learn how to use it — it is much quicker! However, do it twice as a check.

(iii) More men in 1951   1
Higher average age in 1951   1

Examiner's tip You will also be given credit for other relevant comments, e.g. 'Men lived longer in 1951', 'There were more men over 60 in 1951', etc.

(b) (i) Cumulative frequencies:

	1881	1951
under 15	4740	3785
under 30	8120	7935
under 45	10370	12574
under 60	11800	16296
under 75	12510	18528
under 90	12620	19062

1+1

Question	Answer	Mark

(ii)

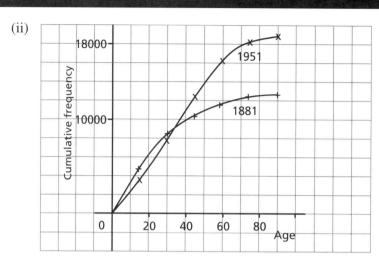

2+2

(1 mark deducted for each mistake)

(c)

	Median	**IQ range**	**% over 21**	
1881	20	38 − 10 = 28	50	1+1+1
1951	35	50 − 20 = 30	73	1+1+1

Examiner's tip Read medians at half total frequency (6310/9531). Read quartiles at 25%/75% of total frequency (3155/9465, 4765/14 296). Subtract readings at 21 years from total frequency and convert to percentages.

(d) Fewer young men in 1951 (% under 21)   1
Greater spread of ages (interquartile range greater) in 1951   1

Examiner's tip There are other possible comments but make sure yours are different from the earlier part. This question is longer than you would be expected to do under examination conditions. In an examination, you would probably not have to repeat calculations, as here, but these were included for practice.

*6 (a)   A–C–I–G   1

Examiner's tip This is the path through the network which takes the longest time. Any delay in any of these tasks will delay completion.

(b)   5 + 8 + 5 + 2 = 20 days   1

Examiner's tip This is the total time along the critical path.

(c)   A–C–I–G: 1 person   1
F–E: 1 person   1
Second person has 8 days left and can complete J–D and B–H   1

Question	Answer	Mark

Examiner's tip Notice that the second person cannot start J until day 14. He/she must therefore do B (or H) as well before moving to J and D.

---

*7 (a) $s > e, e \geqslant 8$ 1+1

(b) $300s + 500e \leqslant 9000$ 1

(c)

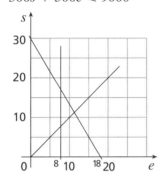

     3
(1 for each line)

    (i) 16   (ii) 11   1+1

(d) 9 executive and 15 small, giving £2 055 000.   2

Examiner's tip Care is needed in solving this problem as only points with integer coordinates can be used. Nobody wants 0.6 of a house! If in doubt, try other points and find the totals for them.

---

8 (a) $\dfrac{4}{52} = \dfrac{1}{13}$ 1

(b) $\dfrac{2}{40} = \dfrac{1}{20}$ 1

Examiner's tip Decimal answers are also acceptable, but not ratios or statements such as '1 out of 13'.

9 (a) $0.25 + 0.5 = 0.75$ 2

(b) $0.25 + 0.125 = 0.375$ 2

(c) One section contains white and 1.   1
The probability for white and 1 has been added in twice   2

Examiner's tip The condition that needs to be satisfied before probabilities can be added is sometimes referred to as the outcomes being 'mutually exclusive'.

Question	Answer	Mark
10 (a)	1,1; 1,2; 1,3; 1,4; 1,5; 1,6; 2,1; 2,2; 2,3; 2,4; 2,5; 2,6; 3,1; 3,2; 3,3; 3,4; 3,5; 3,6; 4,1; 4,2; 4,3; 4,4; 4,5; 4,6.	2

> **Examiner's tip** The order is important. 1 on the first and 2 on the second is a different outcome from 2 on the first and 1 on the second.

(b)

	1	2	3	4	5	6
1	2	3	4	5	6	7
2	3	4	5	6	7	8
3	4	5	6	7	8	9
4	5	6	7	8	9	10

2

(c) (i) $\frac{1}{6}$ (ii) $\frac{12}{24} = \frac{1}{2}$ **1+1**

(d) 5 is also an odd number so the outcomes are not mutually exclusive.   **1**

(e) If the sum is even it is not odd so the probability is $1 - \frac{1}{2} = \frac{1}{2}$ **1**

> **Examiner's tip** The probability of something not happening is 1− (the probability of it happening).

11 (a) $\frac{92}{195}$ (b) $\frac{16+4}{195} = \frac{20}{195} = \frac{4}{39}$ **1+2**

> **Examiner's tip** Since the total number of calls is not given in this question you may assume that it is 195, that is that each call was for only one emergency service.

12 (a) (i)

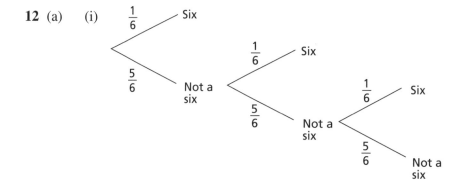

2

Question	Answer	Mark

(ii) $\dfrac{5}{6} \times \dfrac{1}{6}$ — 1

$= \dfrac{5}{36}$ — 1

(iii) Probability he wins = 1 − (probability he does not win) — 1

$$= 1 - \left(\dfrac{5}{6}\right)^{3}$$ — 1

$$= \dfrac{91}{216} \text{ or } 0.421$$ — 1

Examiner's tip Notice that the last part can be calculated from the probability he wins first throw, or the probability he wins second throw, or the probability he wins third throw, i.e.,

$$\dfrac{1}{6} + \dfrac{5}{6} \times \dfrac{1}{6} + \dfrac{5}{6} \times \dfrac{5}{6} \times \dfrac{1}{6}$$

(b)   (i)

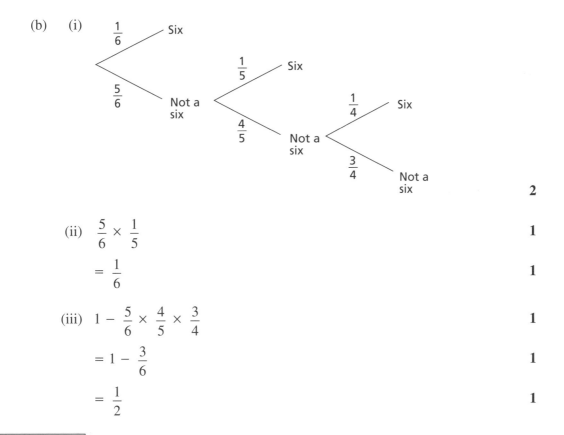

2

(ii) $\dfrac{5}{6} \times \dfrac{1}{5}$ — 1

$= \dfrac{1}{6}$ — 1

(iii) $1 - \dfrac{5}{6} \times \dfrac{4}{5} \times \dfrac{3}{4}$ — 1

$= 1 - \dfrac{3}{6}$ — 1

$= \dfrac{1}{2}$ — 1

Examiner's tip The argument is the same as in part (a) except that conditional probabilities are used because the cards are not replaced. Note that you may have answered parts (iii) and (iv) the other way round.

(iv) As 3 cards are drawn, the probability that they contain the six is $\dfrac{3}{6} = \dfrac{1}{2}$. — 1

Question	Answer	Mark
*13	Probability of at least one head = $1 - $ (probability of no head)	1
	Probability of no head in n tosses $= (0.5)^n$	1
	$1 - (0.5)^n > 0.95$	1
	$(0.5)^n < 0.05$	1
	$(0.5)^4 < 0.625$, $(0.5)^5 < 0.03125$, so $n = 5$	1